# 10 Ways to Successfully Work from Home in 2024-25

Working from home has become a prominent aspect of the modern workforce, with many organizations embracing remote work as a permanent fixture.

As technology continues to evolve and work culture adapts, successfully working from home requires a combination of effective strategies, tools, and habits.

Here are ten comprehensive ways to ensure success while working from home in 2024-25.

# 1. **Establish a Dedicated Workspace**

Creating a dedicated workspace is crucial for productivity and focus.

This space should be separate from areas associated with leisure activities.

Here's how to establish an effective workspace:

## a. Choose the Right Location:

Select a quiet corner of your home with minimal distractions.

Ideally, this should be a room with a door you can close to shut out noise and interruptions.

## b. Invest in Ergonomic Furniture:

A comfortable chair and a desk at the right height can prevent back pain and other physical discomforts.

Ergonomic furniture promotes better posture and reduces the risk of repetitive strain injuries.

### c. Personalize Your Space:

Personal touches can make your workspace more inviting.

Add plants, artwork, or anything that inspires you, but avoid clutter which can be distracting.

## d. Ensure Proper Lighting:

Good lighting is essential to reduce eye strain.

Natural light is ideal, but if that's not possible, invest in quality artificial lighting that mimics daylight.

### e. Equip with Necessary Tools:

Make sure your workspace is equipped with all the tools you need, such as a computer, high-speed internet, printer, and any specific equipment relevant to your job.

## 2. Maintain a Routine

A structured routine can mimic the discipline of an office environment, which is key for productivity.

### a. Set Regular Working Hours:

Consistency helps your body and mind get into a work rhythm.

Stick to a schedule similar to your office hours to maintain work-life balance.

## b. Morning Routine:

Start your day with a morning routine similar to what you would do if you were going to the office.

This could include a shower, breakfast, and a few minutes of relaxation or exercise.

## c. Plan Your Day:

Begin each day by creating a to-do list.

Prioritize tasks and set realistic goals for what you want to achieve.

## d. Take Breaks:

Regular breaks are crucial to avoid burnout.

Use techniques like the Pomodoro Technique, where you work for 25 minutes and then take a 5-minute break.

## e. End Your Day with a Routine:

Just as you start your day with a routine, end it with one too.

This could involve shutting down your computer, clearing your workspace, and engaging in a relaxing activity.

## 3. Leverage Technology

Technology plays a significant role in remote work, facilitating communication, collaboration, and productivity.

**a. Communication Tools:**

Utilize tools like Slack, Microsoft Teams, or Zoom for effective communication.

Regular check-ins and virtual meetings can help maintain team cohesion.

## b. Project Management Software:

Tools like Trello, Asana, and Monday.com can help you keep track of tasks, deadlines, and team collaboration.

## c. Cloud Storage:

Use cloud storage services such as Google Drive, Dropbox, or OneDrive for easy access to documents and collaborative work.

### d. Time Management Apps:

Apps like Toggl or RescueTime can help you track how you spend your time, identify productivity bottlenecks, and manage your work hours better.

### e. Cybersecurity Measures:

Protect your work with reliable antivirus software, VPNs for secure connections, and regular backups to prevent data loss.

# 4. Communication and Collaboration

Effective communication and collaboration are critical in a remote work environment.

## a. Regular Meetings:

Schedule regular team meetings to discuss progress, address issues, and maintain a sense of team spirit.

Video calls can be more engaging than emails or messages.

## b. Clear Communication Channels:

Establish clear communication channels and protocols.

This includes deciding on the primary mode of communication (email, messaging apps, etc.) and setting expectations for response times.

## c. Documentation:

Keep thorough documentation of projects, processes, and decisions.

This ensures that everyone is on the same page and can refer back to documents when needed.

### d. Collaborative Tools:

Use tools like Google Docs or Microsoft Office 365 for real-time collaboration on documents and spreadsheets.

### e. Social Interaction:

Encourage informal social interactions among team members.

Virtual coffee breaks or team-building activities can help build rapport and prevent feelings of isolation.

## 5. Time Management and Productivity

Managing time effectively is a cornerstone of successful remote work.

### a. Prioritize Tasks:

Identify your most important tasks and tackle them first.

Use techniques like the Eisenhower Matrix to categorize tasks based on urgency and importance.

### b. Avoid Multitasking:

Focus on one task at a time to improve the quality of your work and reduce mistakes.

### c. Set Boundaries:

Establish clear boundaries with family or housemates regarding your work hours and space to minimize interruptions.

## d. Use Productivity Techniques:

Techniques like time blocking, where you dedicate specific blocks of time to different tasks, can help you stay focused and productive.

## e. Monitor Progress:

Regularly review your progress against your goals and adjust your strategies as needed to stay on track.

# 6. Health and Well-being

Maintaining physical and mental health is essential when working from home.

## a. Exercise Regularly:

Incorporate physical activity into your daily routine.

This could be a morning jog, a midday yoga session, or evening stretches.

## b. Healthy Eating:

Eat balanced meals and stay hydrated.

Avoid the temptation of frequent snacking on unhealthy foods.

### c. Mental Health:

 Practice mindfulness, meditation, or other relaxation techniques to manage stress.

 Don't hesitate to seek professional help if you're feeling overwhelmed.

## d. Social Connections:

 Stay connected with friends and family.

 Social interactions are important for mental well-being, even if they are virtual.

### e. Work-Life Balance:

Avoid overworking by setting clear boundaries between work and personal time.

Ensure you take time to relax and pursue hobbies or activities you enjoy.

# 7. Professional Development

Continued learning and professional growth should not be neglected while working remotely.

## a. Online Courses:

Enroll in online courses to learn new skills or improve existing ones.

Platforms like Coursera, Udemy, and LinkedIn Learning offer a wide range of courses.

### b. Webinars and Workshops:

Attend virtual webinars and workshops to stay updated with industry trends and network with other professionals.

### c. Certifications:

Pursue relevant certifications that can enhance your qualifications and career prospects.

### d. Reading:

Regularly read industry-related books, articles, and journals to stay informed and inspired.

### e. Mentorship:

Seek out a mentor or become one yourself.

Mentoring relationships can provide valuable insights and support for professional growth.

# 8. Personal Accountability and Self-Motivation

Working from home requires a high level of personal accountability and self-motivation.

## a. Set Personal Goals:

Establish short-term and long-term goals for your work.

Having clear objectives can help you stay focused and motivated.

## b. Track Your Progress:

Use tools like journals, spreadsheets, or apps to track your progress and reflect on your achievements and areas for improvement.

## c. Reward Yourself:

Recognize and reward your accomplishments, no matter how small.

This can help maintain motivation and a positive attitude.

## d. Stay Disciplined:

Stick to your routines and schedules even when it's challenging.

Discipline is key to maintaining productivity and achieving your goals.

e. Seek Feedback:

Regularly seek feedback from colleagues, supervisors, and clients.

Constructive feedback can provide insights into areas where you can improve and help you stay on track.

## 9. Embrace Flexibility

One of the advantages of working from home is the ability to have a flexible schedule.

**a. Flexible Hours:**

If your job allows, work during the hours when you are most productive, whether that's early in the morning or late at night.

## b. Balance Work and Personal Life:

Use the flexibility to balance work responsibilities with personal commitments, such as family time, exercise, and hobbies.

## c. Adapt to Changes:

Be prepared to adapt to changes in your work environment or routine.

Flexibility can help you navigate unexpected challenges more effectively.

### d. Experiment with Work Styles:

Try different work styles and routines to find what works best for you.

This might include varying your work location, using different productivity techniques, or adjusting your work hours.

## e. Take Advantage of Remote Opportunities:

Embrace opportunities that remote work offers, such as the ability to travel while working or the chance to pursue additional freelance projects.

## 10. Cultivate a Positive Work Environment

A positive work environment can significantly impact your motivation and productivity.

### a. Positive Mindset:

Cultivate a positive mindset by focusing on the benefits of remote work, such as flexibility and the ability to create a personalized work environment.

## b. Stay Organized:

Keep your workspace and digital files organized.

An organized environment can reduce stress and improve efficiency.

## c. Set Realistic Expectations:

Set realistic expectations for yourself and communicate them to your team.

Avoid overcommitting and ensure you have the resources to meet your goals.

## d. Build Strong Relationships:

Foster strong relationships with your colleagues through effective communication and collaboration.

A supportive team can enhance job satisfaction and productivity.

### e. Continuous Improvement:

Regularly assess your work habits and environment, and look for ways to improve.

Small changes can have a significant impact on your overall work experience.

## **Conclusion**

Successfully working from home in 2024-25 involves a combination of establishing a dedicated workspace, maintaining a routine, leveraging technology, effective communication, time management, prioritizing health and well-being, focusing on professional development, personal accountability, embracing flexibility, and cultivating a positive work environment.

By implementing these strategies, you can enhance your productivity, maintain work-life balance, and thrive in a remote work setting.

As the nature of work continues to evolve, these practices will remain essential for achieving success while working from home.

Please use the next few pages for your notes and debates.

www.ingramcontent.com/pod-product-compliance
Lightning Source LLC
Chambersburg PA
CBHW072000210526
45479CB00003B/1006